STATES OF MATTER

BY MARIE ROESSER

Please visit our website, www.enslow.com.
For a free color catalog of all our high-quality books, call toll free
1-800-398-2504 or fax 1-877-980-4454.

Library of Congress Cataloging-in-Publication Data

Names: Roesser, Marie, author.
Title: States of matter / Marie Roesser.
Description: New York : Enslow Publishing, [2026] | Series: Chemistry in review | Includes bibliographical references and index.
Identifiers: LCCN 2024037415 (print) | LCCN 2024037416 (ebook) | ISBN 9781978542945 (library binding) | ISBN 9781978542938 (paperback) | ISBN 9781978542952 (ebook)
Subjects: LCSH: Matter–Properties–Juvenile literature. | Matter–Juvenile literature.
Classification: LCC QC173.36 .R64 2026 (print) | LCC QC173.36 (ebook) | DDC 530.4–dc23/eng/20241112
LC record available at https://lccn.loc.gov/2024037415
LC ebook record available at https://lccn.loc.gov/2024037416

Published in 2026 by
Enslow Publishing
2544 Clinton Street
Buffalo, NY 14224

Copyright © 2026 Enslow Publishing

Portions of this work were originally authored by Mary Griffin and published as *States of Matter* (A Look at Chemistry). All new material in this edition is authored by Marie Roesser.

Designer: Claire Zimmermann
Editor: Therese Shea

Photo credits: Cover, p. 1 (main image) Butusova Elena/Shutterstock.com; series art (molecule header image) jijomathaidesigners/Shutterstock.com; p. 5 Sunny studio/Shutterstock.com; p. 9 Dima Zel/Shutterstock.com; p. 15 (copper) Adwo/Shutterstock.com; p. 17 New Africa/Shutterstock.com; p. 19 Raland/Shutterstock.com; p. 21 MarcelClemens/Shutterstock.com; p. 25 VectorMine/Shutterstock.com; p. 27 (top) Triff/Shutterstock.com, (bottom) Hasantha Lakmal/Shutterstock.com; p. 29 Nutchapong Wuttisak/Shutterstock.com.

All rights reserved. No part of this book may be reproduced in any form without permission in writing from the publisher, except by a reviewer.

Printed in China

Some of the images in this book illustrate individuals who are models. The depictions do not imply actual situations or events.

CPSIA compliance information: Batch #QSENS26: For further information contact Enslow Publishing, at 1-800-398-2504.

CONTENTS

It's All Matter.............................4

Atoms Are the Answer.............8

Inside Solids..........................14

Studying Water.......................20

Searching for More States.....26

Four States of Matter.............30

Glossary.................................31

For More Information............32

Index.....................................32

Words in the glossary appear in **bold** the first time they are used in the text.

IT'S ALL MATTER

Matter is everything that takes up space and has **mass**. That's everything around you. You can see and touch matter if it's in the form of solids or liquids. Gases are a state, or form, of matter that you can't see.

🔍 LEARN MORE

Gases have both **volume** and mass, just like solids and liquids do.

Solid, liquid, and gas are the three main states of matter. They're sometimes called phases of matter too. You can see these states every day in water. Liquid water can turn into solid ice. Water also has a gas form called water vapor.

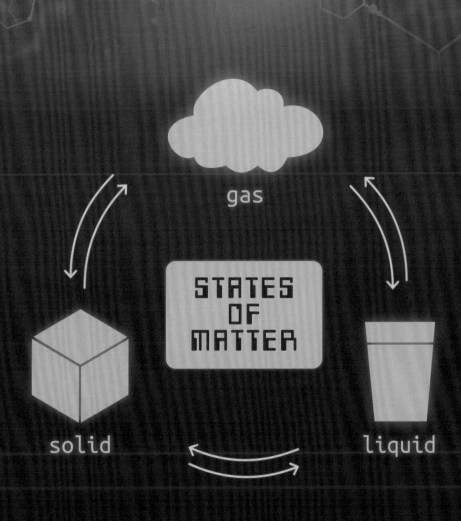

🔍 LEARN MORE

You can't see water vapor. Steam and fog are drops of liquid water mixed with water vapor. It's the drops that you see.

ATOMS ARE THE ANSWER

We know **substances** change forms. But why do they? We need to look at the atoms that combine to form them. Atoms are the smallest parts of elements, which are the building blocks of matter. There are 118 known kinds of elements, and so there are 118 different kinds of atoms.

🔍 LEARN MORE

Carbon, oxygen, and gold are some elements you might know. An atom of these and all elements are so small we can't see them with our eyes.

Some substances in nature, such as the element helium, are made up of single atoms. But most are made up of groups of atoms called molecules. Molecules with more than one kind of element are called compounds. Molecules can be countless sizes and shapes.

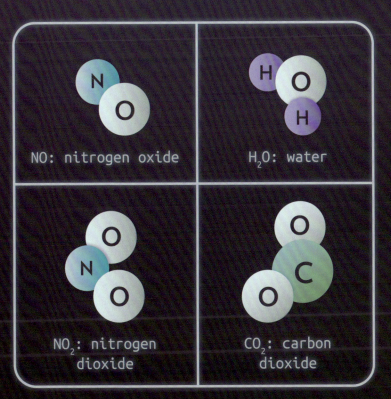

🔍 LEARN MORE

Elements are often marked as letters in molecule models and **chemical formulas**. This image shows elements above the table and compounds (molecules of different elements) in the table.

Temperature and **pressure** can cause changes in atoms and molecules. These changes can cause the state of matter to change. Whether or not matter changes can depend on where atoms are in a molecule, how they're moving, and the strength of their attraction, or draw, to other atoms.

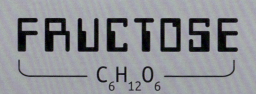

FRUCTOSE
$C_6H_{12}O_6$

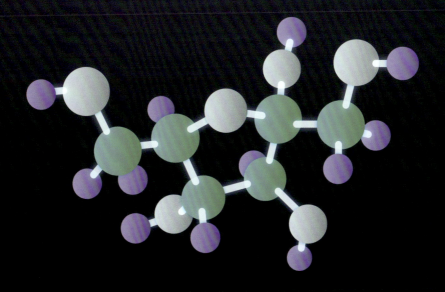

 oxygen   hydrogen   carbon

🔍 LEARN MORE

Molecules are in motion. The atoms within them turn and shake too. They can look even more **complex** than this molecule, a kind of sugar.

13

INSIDE SOLIDS

At room temperature, just two elements are liquid, eleven are gases, and the rest are solids. In solid matter, molecules are packed tightly together. They have a strong attraction to each other. That's why solids hold a certain shape.

SOLID STRUCTURES

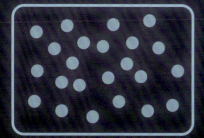
amorphous solids

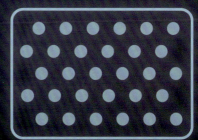
crystalline solids

copper

🔍 LEARN MORE

A crystalline solid has a pattern of atoms or molecules. Most metal elements, including copper, are crystalline at room temperature. Solids that aren't as ordered are called amorphous.

Molecules in a solid are packed together but still have space between them. In a liquid, molecules have even more space between them. They're attracted to each other but can move around. That's why liquids can be poured. Liquids take the shape of the container they fill.

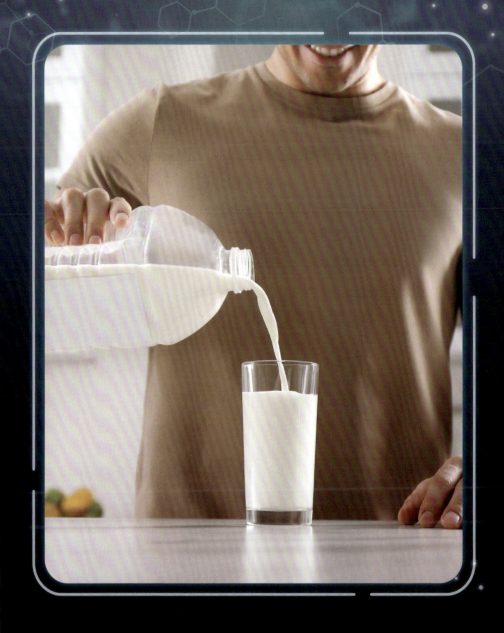

🔍 LEARN MORE

A liquid's volume doesn't change when it's in another container.

17

When a liquid turns to a gas, its molecules move farther apart. They're not close enough to be attracted to each other. They move at high speeds. A gas will **expand** and fill any container. Gases can also be **compressed** to take up less volume.

🔍 LEARN MORE

A gas's volume changes with the volume of its container.

STUDYING WATER

You know the **physical** effects of temperature on water. Let's take a closer look at water molecules as they undergo these changes. Water is the only matter naturally found in gas, liquid, and solid form on our planet. It can help us understand how other matter changes forms.

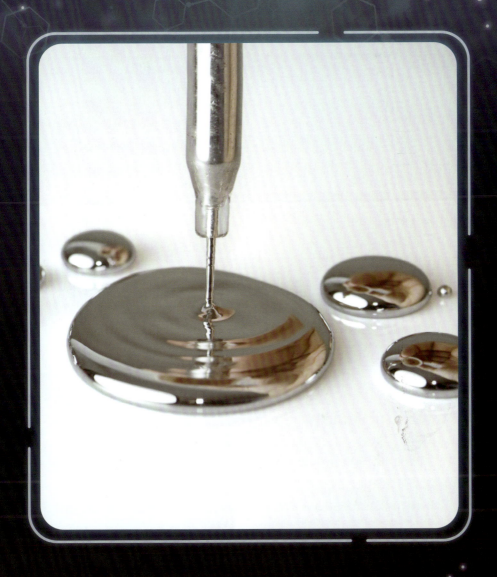

🔍 LEARN MORE

Scientists have found ways to make matter other than water change states. Mercury, a metal at room temperature, can be turned into a solid when cooled to -37.9°F (-38.8°C).

When temperatures rise, molecules in liquid water move around more. If the temperature is high enough, the liquid changes into water vapor. This is called evaporating or vaporizing. But if the temperature is cold enough, molecules in liquid water slow and attract. Water freezes to become solid ice.

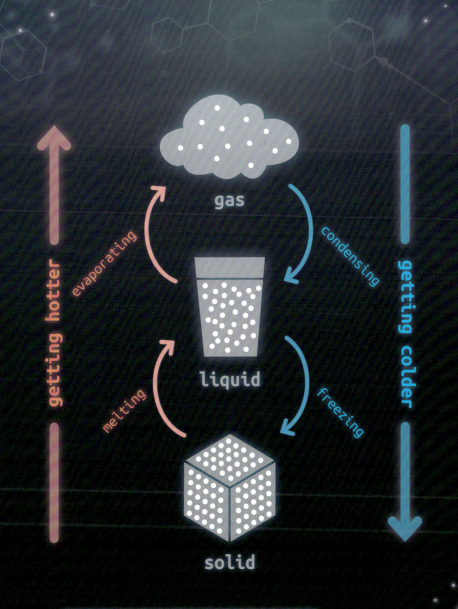

LEARN MORE

When water vapor cools, the gas can condense, or turn into liquid. Ice can become a gas without turning into a liquid first. This is called sublimation.

Pressure can also cause water to change states. Pressure from Earth's **atmosphere** is greater at sea level than in the mountains. In the mountains, water boils—and changes into gas—at a lower temperature than at sea level!

BOILING POINT OF WATER

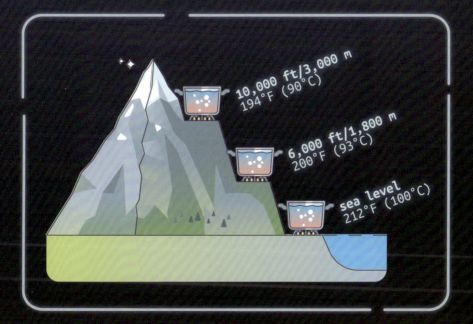

🔍 LEARN MORE

Great pressure and high temperature deep within Earth causes solids to become liquids. That's how liquid rock, or magma, forms.

SEARCHING
FOR MORE STATES

Plasma occurs at superhot temperatures. Tiny bits called **electrons** are knocked off atoms as they fly around. Some consider this a special **ionized** gas. Others think it's another state of matter. Lightning is an example of plasma in nature. The element neon becomes plasma when heated with electricity.

🔍 LEARN MORE

Plasma is used for some signs and TVs. It's not as common on Earth, but scientists think about 99 percent of the universe is in the plasma state!

In 1995, scientists created another state of matter in a lab. They cooled about 2,000 atoms of a gas to almost **absolute zero**. The atoms hardly moved and acted like a single "superatom." The scientists called this state of matter Bose-Einstein condensate. Will other states of matter be found?

🔍 LEARN MORE

It's important to remember that states of matter don't cause a chemical change in substances, just a physical change.

FOUR STATES OF MATTER

  heating →

SOLID

LIQUID

GAS

PLASMA

← cooling

SOLID	LIQUID	GAS	PLASMA
strong bond	weak bond	no bond	ionization
regular arrangement	irregular arrangement	irregular arrangement	irregular arrangement
vibrates almost in fixed position	moves around each other	moves in all directions	moves in all directions
rigid	takes container's shape	not rigid	has definite shape
fixed volume	fixed volume	not fixed volume	not fixed volume

30

GLOSSARY

absolute zero: The temperature believed to be the lowest possible temperature. It's about $-459.67\,°F$ ($-273.15\,°C$).

atmosphere: The mixture of gases that surround a planet.

chemical formula: A series of letters, numbers, and symbols showing the chemicals that a molecule or compound is made of.

complex: Having to do with something with many parts that work together.

compress: To press or squeeze together.

electron: A particle found in atoms that acts as a carrier of electricity in solids.

expand: To get larger and looser.

ionized: Having atoms or groups of atoms that have a positive or negative electric charge from losing or gaining one or more electrons.

mass: The amount of matter in an object.

physical: Having to do with a form you can touch or see, such as the body.

pressure: A force that pushes on something else.

substance: A certain kind of matter.

temperature: How hot or cold something is.

volume: The amount of space an object takes up.

FOR MORE INFORMATION

BOOKS

Faust, Daniel R. *States of Matter*. Minneapolis, MN: Bearport Publishing Company, 2023.

Mullins, Matt. *Investigating States of Matter*. Ann Arbor, MI: Cherry Lake Publishing, 2024.

WEBSITE

What Are the States of Matter?
www.bbc.co.uk/bitesize/articles/zsgwwxs
Check out this review, and then take a quiz.

INDEX

Bose-Einstein condensate, 28
compounds, 10, 11
elements, 8, 9, 10, 11, 14, 15, 26
ice, 6, 22, 23
mass, 4, 5

phases, 6
plasma, 26, 27
pressure, 12, 24, 25
temperature, 12, 14, 15, 20, 21, 22, 24, 25, 26
vapor, 6, 7, 22, 23
volume, 5, 17, 18, 19